Render

Collin Kelley

Poems

Alexander, Arkansas
www.siblingrivalrypress.com

Render

Copyright © 2013 by Collin Kelley.

Cover photograph by Colin Potts.

Author photo by Colin Potts.

Cover design by Mona Z. Kraculdy.

The typeset is Book Antiqua.

All rights reserved. No part of this book may be reproduced or republished without written consent from the publisher, except by reviewers who may quote brief excerpts in connection with a review in a newspaper, magazine, or electronic publication; nor may any part of this book be reproduced, stored in a retrieval system, or transmitted in any form, or by any means be recorded without written consent of the publisher.

Sibling Rivalry Press, LLC
13913 Magnolia Glen Drive
Alexander, AR 72002

www.siblingrivalrypress.com
info@siblingrivalrypress.com

ISBN: 978-1-937420-34-5

Library of Congress Control Number: 2012951646

First Sibling Rivalry Press Edition, April 2013

For my parents

Contents

reticulation

A Broken Frame — 13

aperture

Blackout	17
Freedom Train	18
Wonder Woman	19
Funtown	20
Breaking My Mother's Leg	21
Barney Rubble Saves Our Lives	22
Tuscumbia, Alabama	24
Three Mile Island	26
Squelch	27
Parallel Lines	28
To Margot Kidder, With Love	29
First Blackmail	31
After Adultery	32
At Southlake Mall	33
Knoxville: Summer, 1982	34
Physical Education	35
Members Only	36
Blowing Rock, NC	37
Trivial Pursuits	38
First Gay Crush	39
Ian	40
Stroke	41
In Stockholm	43
My Mother Demonstrates How To Escape From A Plane Crash	44

blowup

Detour	47
Sex In My Parents' House	48
Bare Back	49
Hustling	50
Mr. Rogers Made Me Fat	51
Freshman Orientation	52
Post	53
Sex Machines	54
After You Left	55
Garland	56
Night 65	57
Girl Crush	58
The Virgin Mary Appears in a Highway Underpass	59
Why I Want To Be Pam Grier	60
Confirmed Bachelor	61
Raise the Titanic	62
Christmas Day	63
Broken Things	64
My Father Escapes A London Hotel Fire	65

resolution

Render	69

Render

reticulation

A Broken Frame

The photograph has no date,
but these are my long-ago kin,
ancestors just before the boat,
six stone-faced on the English shore,
sepia on cardstock under glass
still clear in severe, dark clothes
except one who has been marked
out, maybe with black wax,
which runs to the bottom corner
where the frame is cracked.

Did he die in transit, get lettered
for adultery on that long crossing,
gamble away starting-over money,
or was he the child they could no
longer bear, the ruin of the family?
The one who kissed other boys,
should have been left behind,
whose black ghost gave up
the dream, slipped out of the picture
through a broken place, a sliver.

aperture

Blackout

I could have been a blackout baby
if geography hadn't conspired
to keep lights on below the Mason-Dixon line,
my parents coupling in the fall of 1965,
but it would be four more years before
I came squalling into their lives.

I wasn't a gleam in anyone's eye,
my father avoiding Vietnam to come home
to my mother who wrote soppy diary entries
to convince herself of happiness.
Too many *I miss him's*, too many *lonely nights*.

Words ended when he returned, white vistas
of empty pages, as if she died mid-sentence,
suddenly discovered marriage,
her eloquent pining away perfected
for lunch and shopping with girlfriends
shimmering away, stilling pen and childhood.

January 1969, the doctor's pronouncement
surprising as power failure.
I'd come in September on the anniversary
of the Battle of Antietam, her belly
hardly showing my existence.
I wonder if she wished '65 back at the final push?
That wild center of a decade, before responsibility
and madness turned out the lights.

Freedom Train

What did we do July 4, 1976?
I have no memory of that Bicentennial overload,
a hysterical red, white and blue frenzy.
We were living in a dark, rented house
on the outskirts of town, just a year away
from my mother's affair and my father's blind eye.
I was jumping off beds like the Bionic Woman,
besotted with Farrah's red bathing suit,
wanting to know why Atlanta burned
with *Gone With the Wind* on TV for the first time.

Vietnam, Watergate, gas shortages, economic woes
totally passed me by. We were poor and living
in our own slowly escalating war zone:
Mother's brooding unhappiness, Dad's work ethic
keeping him out of the house and underpaid.

What I really remember about that year
was wanting to see the Freedom Train.
It pulled into rail yards, a traveling museum
of Americana. I couldn't tell you the exhibits.
I only wanted to see one thing: the ruby red slippers
Dorothy wore in *The Wizard of Oz*.
They gleamed like the Hope Diamond
under a cheap light bulb.
I could have stood there all day, but guides ushered us
through, not understanding how much I needed
those shoes to click my way out of the coming storm,
the dread I already felt at age six.

Maybe we saw fireworks on Independence Day,
stood on the sidelines of the pathetic parade
that slogged through humidity, led by dispirited
baton girls and sweating politicians riding in open cars.
Maybe I was looking skyward, waiting
for that plume of smoke that would spell doom,
like when the Wicked Witch came and wrote
words across the horizon: *Surrender Dorothy*.

Wonder Woman

The day I told my parents I wanted to trade in
G.I. Joe for Wonder Woman must have set off alarms.
I wanted to surrender my guns for the golden lasso;
more than the dolls, mind you, I wanted to *be*
Wonder Woman.
I don't remember who stitched the costume:
blue underwear with glued-on stars, a red bustier
wrapped around my seven-year-old sunken chest,
the golden eagle oddly deflated,
the head band and bullet deflecting cuffs made
of cardboard and the length of rope my father had
spray-painted gold in the yard hooked at my side.
I lassoed my poor dad first, demanded the truth,
but there was no magic in those rough, twisted fibers.
If the rope could have squeezed out an ounce
of what he was really thinking,
I would have been dressed up as Superman or Batman,
a manly cape flying out behind me as I ran
around the backyard, hidden from the neighbors,
while my dad devised a way to build
Wonder Woman's invisible plane.

Funtown

Abandoned putt-putt golf course
on a street that will eventually
become prostitute stroll –
a picture of me at age five
hugging the flaking remains
of a dinosaur on the fourth green.
Pre-historic houses choked
with weeds, Astroturf buckling
and bleached, water feature
gone dry before I was born.
My parents say the photo
does not exist,
that I've confused this memory
with one of my Uncle Terry,
our last visit before he packed
up and moved to San Francisco
with his boyfriend, before AIDS,
before *memento mori* meant
anything to him, or me. I am
certain I was there, squinting
in the glare, a double image
splitting us in half, the halo
of sun spots transferring
the life he would not finish
on to me so seamlessly
I misremember where our lives intersect,
synapses carving: *I was here.*

Breaking My Mother's Leg

Just off the back porch,
I splashed happily in my kiddie pool
until a Godzilla-sized grasshopper
jumped in to enjoy a summer soak.

After my scream pierced the humid air,
my mother burst through the screen door
and dove from the top step.
The judges would have given her 10s
for her somersault over the shallow water,
but she couldn't stick the landing.

When I recovered, my mother
was half-in, half-out of the pool,
reclining like a bathing beauty,
but then I saw her right leg, twisted
at an unnatural angle, and her smile of relief
that I had not drowned turned to frown
as her eyes followed mine.

She would wear a cast to her thigh
for the rest of the summer, perfecting invalid,
and she would never be the same again.
After mending, she lived a lifetime in five years,
casting my father off for another man,
flaunting herself around town.

The sharp crack of bones
was a dividing line between one life and the next,
a grace period before a host of maladies set in —
ruptured ulcers, impacted teeth and crippling stroke —
a storm that never rained itself out.

Barney Rubble Saves Our Lives

I am seven and *The Flintstones* are my obsession,
a molded, plastic bank in the shape of diminutive
Barney Rubble, his jovial smile, flaxen hair,
dildo nose, carried in my arms like a graven image.

High on Brasstown Bald, twilight arrives
unexpectedly, my father urging my mother
and me back into the puke-green Ford LTD
for the trip back down the mountain,
the observatory parking lot empty.
For the first time, I understand dread
as my father turns over the engine,
and smoke curls from under the hood.

We all sit there, momentary brain drain,
flash-forwarding on darkness, cold,
spending the night in the car, Big Foot.
My father springs to action, pulls
dipsticks, tugs wires, nose sharp for leaks.

He diagnoses busted radiator hose,
and as if by magic, a thin trail of fluid
appears and flows downhill, away from us,
fleeing approaching night.
My father remembers a gas station,
says we'll make it if we can fill up the radiator,
but my mother's frantic search is fruitless:
no cups, no thermos, no cooler to carry water
from the primitive fountain.

That's when I offer up Barney,
remove the flesh colored cap from his feet,
place my finger over the change slot in his head,
make him prehistoric vessel.

Even after I lose interest, Barney remains,
not tossed into dark attic or tagged for yard sale,
but tucked into a corner of the trunk, and since
Hanna-Barbera never gave him a proper job,
we keep him employed, our tiny lifesaver.

Tuscumbia, Alabama

My dad at the wheel, my mother's ulcer inflamed, she puked her way across northern Alabama that summer, from Huntsville and the rusting rockets to Tuscumbia, the farthest any of us had been west. We drove through raw, blistered towns, like a hundred Sally Mann photos come to life, the hollow-eyed poor, the rust and dust. Helen Keller would have wished herself blind.

My parents on each end of a see-saw, up and down, and me in the middle, a counterbalance. My mother said more than once, *I want to leave*. In the hush after battle, when only a book was a safe bet, I found poor Helen. Wondered how she managed happiness in her turncoat body, how Annie Sullivan's urgent fingers slapped against Helen's young hand could make three senses seem like five.

At Ivy Green, the Kellers' low slung house, I thought I came to find Helen but was looking for Annie, the surrogate mother who rescued Helen from her lock box. Who suffered the sadistic mind-games, thrown forks and eggs, lost a tooth for her trouble, who resolved to stay until water became water. Half-blind herself, her thick glasses like mine, learning Braille just in case. Her brother dead in an orphanage she barely managed to escape. She didn't want to leave him either; his apparition showed her the door.

Alabama in 1881 must have been a fresh hell, Annie's Yankee hostility a constant reminder of who had won the War of Northern Aggression. The Kellers giving in to Helen's every whim was a new battleground, yet Annie never yielded. The high, hot southern sun scorching her corneas even after the surgeries, books held so close her eyelashes rustled the pages, hungry to absorb every visible word, to ingrain them in case she woke up in permanent darkness. Going back to Boston was never an option.

My mother's insides finally settled, she stared out the window of Ivy Green, looking into some middle distance, beyond my father into the next life of no children, no responsibilities, a clean slate to begin again. I picked up Helen's Braille watch, the one lost in NYC and returned by a stranger, because who else would it belong to but her, as if no one else in the world was blind. I wondered where Annie's watch was now, the one I'm sure she picked up a million times and said, *I want to leave, get off this see-saw.* Could have. Did not.

Three Mile Island

I still dream of those snowy white smokestacks,
permanent mushroom clouds.
The way the news cameras caught them in the flaming
sunrise over the Susquehanna. It was late March,
but when I remember the meltdown, it seems like summer.
Maybe it was that fear of being cooked or the earth
opening up and sinking us all to China.
I wanted to be there, wearing plaid pants, wide collar
jacket and Dad's Vitalis slicking back my hair.
Wanted that microphone, puffed like cotton candy
against my lips in near hysteria at the scoop of 1979.
I couldn't sleep for five days, waiting for the hydrogen
bubble to burst and kill us all. Pennsylvania seemed
really close when I was 10 and the doomsday mass
held by the Harrisburg priest didn't help. He offered
general absolution, and I, not even a Catholic,
not having yet set foot in a church, quietly prayed
to be a witness, an Armageddon altar boy.
In school, they used to make you crawl under a desk
with your hands locked over your head, as if this could
save you from the bomb. Fuck that.
If I'm going to be incinerated, I don't want the slow,
leaching death of cancer. I want to be standing
at the window as the flash comes, like those soldiers
at Trinity 1945, sunglasses reflecting a fire that should
have never been conjured, the wind in my hair.

Squelch

Breaker one-nine, breaker one-nine,
staccato slang for speed traps,
Smokey and greasy spoons.
Blame it on Burt and Sally –
sexy in souped-up Trans-Am,
illegal beer, thrill of the hunt.
Hot plastic cupped in hand,
lips pressed close,
my mother's whispery voice
sending the scent of eager beaver
across three counties:
This is Foxy Lady, who's got their ears on?

We let the devil in that day,
antenna rising like a white flag
over boondock house.
My mother's new addiction: a black box
glowing on kitchen counter, hotter than any stove.
Her universe reduced to meters, huddled
in a chair, castaway connected to civilization.
Her static and crackle louder than my father,
his extraneous noise dialed out in the squelch.

We would lose meals and time
in channel-hopping void, disembodied voices
fading in and out of our lives except one,
Desperado, whose voice sent meter into red,
my mother into glittery jittery glee.
Her call and response like Marilyn singing
Happy Birthday every day to dead presidents,
until my father's head snapped back one night,
catching their rock n' roll hoochie coo,
smashing microphone into linoleum.
But by then a strange Camaro was cruising
our twenty and mom was wearing lipstick again.

Parallel Lines

My mother's mother, the one I called Moom Moom so often as a baby that it became her nickname, dances around her kitchen to Blondie singing *Heart of Glass* on the radio. It's 1979 and Debbie and the boys have sold out to disco, but the mainstream doesn't care. Dancers scream whenever the DJ spins it at the clubs, that's what my grandmother says as she teaches me The Hustle on cracked linoleum, her new husband claps along, can't take his eyes off her. Moom Moom is re-married to a trucker, divorced my one-handed, alcoholic grandfather as soon as the nest emptied, tired of the gun in her face, waking up marinated in his drunken piss. She likes long hauls, seeing the world, while my mother turns bitter and adulterous, no sizzle in the bacon my father brings home. I stay up all night to watch Blondie on the *Midnight Special*, learn Debbie's shawl dance with a ripped bed sheet, purloined heels, face smeared with lipstick, sucking a candy cigarette, Mother's whereabouts unknown.

To Margot Kidder, With Love

I spent the summer of 1980 with Margot Kidder,
made her my surrogate on those hot Friday afternoons
when my mother would dump me at the movie theatre,
flying off to her other life faster than Superman.

They all knew me at the counter, asking
for the same ticket every week. I smiled,
perfected my act of comic book geek,
but even those indifferent teenagers had X-ray vision.

In the dark, I mouthed the dialogue
like a Shakespearean tragedy as Margot Kidder
beamed down at me from the undercarriage
of an Eiffel Tower elevator commandeered
by terrorists, jumped into the raging Niagara River,
hung from wires for hours as she pretended to fly.

I pretended not to care what my mother was doing,
but I was cashing in part of my childhood to keep up
the charade as she tucked money in my pocket
for popcorn and a strange phone number
where she could be reached in case of emergency.

Margot Kidder eased me through rising panic
every Friday at 1 p.m. as I was deposited
on the sidewalk, and Mother's car shimmered
like a disappearing mirage, moving bullet time
away from me.

Margot Kidder was Lois Lane.
Feisty, brave, stubborn, in perpetual need of rescue.
Her dark hair, un-PC cigarette dangling,
whiskey voice, in love with the one man
she could never truly have.

Years later, when she had her publicized breakdown,

was found dirty and wandering the streets,
I cried in front of the TV, wishing I could give her
even a fragment of the comfort she gave me
when I was ten and in need of rescue.

First Blackmail

I picked the movie *Absence of Malice*,
liked the way the title rolled off my tongue,
no spite in my heart in 1981.
Tommy was a good sport, but we were bored
and lost in the plot in 10 minutes.
Even perky Sally Field couldn't keep our attention.

We played video games in the lobby
until two girls caught Tommy's eye.
He turned on his Boy Scout charm
like he was going for another badge,
seduced them with his *Missile Command* skills.
They giggled and gawked, ran in and out
of the theater, played hide and seek
until ushers shooed and shushed.

Tommy, dying to transcend upbringing,
hair on his chest at 13, wanted to finger fuck them,
one on each arm, a miniature playboy.
When he suggested getting naked in the bathroom,
the girls turned red and fled, leaving Tommy
to rub his tented shorts, and I offered myself as substitute.
That's when Tommy got righteous, his lost religion
back with a vengeance, stronger than the need to lose cherry,
said he'd tell his mommy I was a pervert,
that I'd be banned from his basement and *Star Wars* toys.
I chanted: "finger fuck, finger fuck, finger fuck"
as I unzipped him in the echoing stall, first blackmail
bouncing off the porcelain.

We rode home in silence in his parents' station wagon,
Tommy wanting to tell, rat out the ungodly,
his mouth opening and closing with silent confession,
while I hummed along to Linda Ronstadt's *Hurt So Bad*
on the radio, my lips testing new vocabulary,
the way the words "absence of malice" rolled off my tongue.

After Adultery

Mother marches down the long driveway,
kicks up dust like the Tasmanian Devil,
rocks spit from under her sure steps.
She carries cutting shears like a rifle
into battle against two monster hedges,
overgrown sentinels, embarrassments
weighing heavily on her empty dance card.
She attacks the first bush with pent up vengeance,
blades flash in midday sun, shorn leaves
tornado around her head until she's swallowed.
Then the hedge becomes space alien,
and I can hear my mother curse it
like Ripley on the *Sulaco*, egging it on,
calling it a bitch like the roots will answer.

The rash appears that night, covers her
entire body, no region left untouched
by bumps and red streaks.
She becomes unhinged, snatches hair
then a snake naked and striking on bathroom floor.
And we, conscripted caretakers, become targets
for her poison, forked tongue as she floats
Ophelia-style in the tub, water simmering,
her eyes fixed and distant,
as if she has finally found the tesseract,
the wrinkle in time, folding space behind her
so we cannot follow, leaving us
with a crazed shadow, a white devil woman.

At Southlake Mall

My parents made up while I was in Spencer's Gifts
examining fart in a can and hopping cocks,
waiting for other boys to finish flipping through
posters of half-naked women and sports cars.
Greasy fingerprints all over Daisy Duke's cleavage
on sale for 1.99 rolled and bagged, long and stiff.

They sat on a bench by a gurgling fountain, holding hands,
making googly eyes and sipping from the same slushie.
Even then, I wondered what she had promised.
What would erase the image of her naked legs
wrapped around another?
The lover sent running with clothes in hand
to his oversexed Camaro, face bloodied, while my father
slapped my mother repeatedly in the bathroom,
so she could see his cuckold departing in dirty mirror.

With unsigned divorce papers on the dining room table,
my parents devolved back to earlier selves,
teenagers in love, giddy with necking, third base diddling.
They couldn't wait to get home, made me eat my giant pretzel
in the backseat, her hand on his thigh as the Ford shuddered
in excess speed.

While they fucked their way back to middle class malaise,
I shot my wad all over Daisy's mid-section, would never
hang her in my room, just roll her wet and sticky under the bed
for future abuse, the same place I kept a shoplifted *People*,
Christopher Atkins bulging from his *Blue Lagoon* loin cloth,
his face and abs wrinkled from my salty spray.

Knoxville: Summer, 1982

100 degrees at the World's Fair
the Sunsphere shimmers
a giant lollipop that loses
its flavor in one lick.

We sit in a cheap motel room
flipping through unfamiliar TV
our sweat-soaked clothes
stiffening in the over-chilled air.

No one speaks.

Her abandoned lover 236 miles away
my mother watches the phone
a pot that will never boil again
reaches for it, then withdraws.

Back home, Bruce jerks off
without me in his dark basement
fantasizes about cocktease Karen
decides my hand is not enough.

Dad wants to see the body farm
bones picked clean of worries
free of cheats, brats and bills
his 43rd birthday goes unmentioned.

That night I dream the Sunsphere
is a Magic 8 Ball in my hand
I shake it hard, but the same message
always floats to the surface:

better not tell you now.

Physical Education
for David

I push my ass back against him,
feel his hand go slack at my throat,
subtle shifting of power as he grows
hard against my tighty-whiteys,
settling into unexplored crack,
we find empty locker room rhythm.

Before the coach returns,
he pinballs off the benches, struggles
into his too-tight Jordache jeans
and cable knit sweater, pre-come
oozing through boxers, a bead
of sweat dangling off his nose.

I stand there watching, pious
in my t-shirt and Fruit of the Looms,
flaccid and un-aroused, lording
over his secret desires coaxed out
from behind year-old bully screen
and titty-twister fingers.

In PE, he will never look at me again,
too busy hiding his sudden boner
from the other boys who jeer,
call him faggot, and I could save him
with one limp wrist, but this is junior high,
and the smell of blood is in the air.

Members Only

The haves and have-nots become clear
in 7th grade when what you wear
is the deciding factor on the rest of your life,
whether you will be "in" or "out,"
or at least "in" enough not to be ridiculed.

The uniform: Members Only jacket
and white Nikes with red swoosh.
Got it? Get 'em – at all costs,
even if your parents sink deeper
into poor house whirlpool.
No JC Penney knock-offs allowed.
Not like that one boy, name long forgotten
because he was banished,
made unworthy of lineage for wearing
a fake, the coveted tag altered
by his mother's bleeding fingers.
These vultures are eagle-eyed,
got the scent for cheap goods.

It's a playground *Sophie's Choice*,
but always go for the jacket
to absorb the flack your feet will take,
nine dollar K-marts, zig-zaggy stripe
only passing for real a mile away.
Keep their eyes above the waist line
to that embroidered calling card hanging
off the pocket, a key to junior high kingdom.
Walk faster, make your feet blur.

Bobby is the only boy who has a leather
Members Only jacket, dark brown, radiating
money and class, the hallway parts the first day
he wears it, gliding over the floor in his shiny new
Nikes, an Icarus destined never to fall.

He is our god.

Blowing Rock, NC

Alison Moyet on MTV singing *Is This Love?*
Across three states and in every hotel,
that English girl's question unanswerable by me.
Maybe my parents know, but they can't stop fighting
about the cost of the hotel room in Blowing Rock,
the overpriced room, the last-minute room,
the only room in town.
My mother always demanded a nice hotel,
the only reason she traveled, to escape
our disintegrating house, the un-cleanable tub,
dark rings and rust stains etched in porcelain.
She would luxuriate in gleaming white convenience,
wallow on soft sheets until the dream was skin deep.

We were on our way to Appomattox
where the Confederacy surrendered,
and I would begin reconstruction,
come back home changed, ready to plunge.
On this vacation, the last I would ever take with my parents,
my father was determined to drive
from one end of Virginia to the other,
to see Chesapeake Bay as if our lives depended on it.
Before we broke apart, before I grew up,
like he could see what was coming, my surrender
to another, the last bit of kid dust blowing away.

Is this love?
Not yet, not for three more months, not until Dirk
shimmers out of a pool, divested of his nerd garments,
pretty and mute, coming toward me like a siren.

Trivial Pursuits

That night over Trivial Pursuit
when I really looked at you for the first time
got the answer wrong drove home
chanting the correct one purposely swallowed
saw your face like a god in the headlights

First Gay Crush

Dirk was the name of my first gay crush,
goddamn how I lusted after that nerdy fuck.
I was 15 almost 16 and he was 18 going on 19,
and I was the prom queen hot for college cock.
His mismatched clothes, ill-fitting jeans, dirty sneakers,
my queer eye for a sexually confused guy already razor sharp.
I was too young to know I had control,
that my aim was true and his was scattershot
from years of strict military parenting.

We would sit in his dorm room
listening to Nina Hagen records
and watching *Doctor Who* on PBS.
I let my hand stray to touch his thigh, rest there
until he flinched as if flicked by holy water.
My father thought Dirk and I were fucking
after he caught me on the phone at 1 a.m.
in the dark living room.
Oh, Daddy, if only.
He would never come out of the closet for me.

Last night, I dreamed I met Dirk again in a coffee shop.
I saw him through the window, dark hair falling over his eyes,
his perfect white teeth a beacon.
I was thin again, like those last two years of high school
when I starved myself better than any cheerleader,
wearing a black coat tight at the waist.
I slid into the booth next to him, and he kissed me, unafraid.
When I woke, all I could think about was the night
I told him I was gay and had fallen in love with someone else.
He gripped the steering wheel and stared straight ahead,
driving us into oncoming headlights.
"What," he screamed. "What do you want me to do about it?"

Ian

Before you made me a witch,
got forced into the basement to pray,
your mother stripping you, whipping you
with a belt in those sure Jesus strokes,
you kissed me once in the backseat,
crouched low, out of my dad's line of sight
in the rearview mirror.
Then you wrote me a note on scrap paper,
scribbled desire in the margins:
I've wanted to kiss you forever.

You would burn these words later like a spy.
On that sticky summer seat, conjoined twins
from brow to ankle bone, this would be the closest
we came to merging, you almost 16, me almost 18,
and I stepped full grown from the jaws of a college boy
who taught me well while he chewed me up and spit me out,
made first seduction a blood sport.

This was only a test, Ian, to see if I could use my power.
Like Valmont, stripping away your virginity, your God blinders.
I hooked you on the first cast, reeled you in,
left you gasping, until your whispered declarations
were intercepted on the downstairs extension.
I cannot remember your mother's face.

The lashes across your pale skin, the marbled bruises
you hid under long sleeves, your cock and balls
whipped for their perversion, the gall of their hardening.
In the end, you would have set me on fire,
brainwashed into suburban righteousness, on your knees
every night until I was suitably demonized.
In the backseat, you kissing me first,
those little pink lips ready to renounce the church
for one night in the wilderness.

Stroke

The car is nose down in the ditch,
traffic slows, honks, but no one stops.
I can see this from the picture window
framed by dusty, fading curtains.
My body, summoned by unknown
telepathy, cannot make sense of how
my mother has managed this accident.

The driveway becomes dreamstate,
I am moving and not moving,
until I am at the driver's door,
my mother seems unhurt but dazed,
her head and eyes roll without focusing,
sharp call of her name, slapping smooth
face, her mouth opens and closes,
no sound, no recognition, no one home.
Gray car, gray upholstery, she
is wearing a gray sweater and slacks,
the sky in sympathy, as if the world
has been sapped of color.

An ambulance and my father appear
as if beamed down from the Enterprise,
and later I'm told that I made the calls,
slipped the tether of consciousness,
ran back to the house, spoke calmly.
I have no memory of this,
just as my mother has no memory
of leaving the supermarket.
How she got from aisle four
to a hospital room, unable to speak
or move her right side.

I was at the window before her car
went off the road. I can see it
in Zapruder-style slow motion,
my mother looking at me,
her head snapping back, then
letting go of the wheel.

In Stockholm

When she can walk again without assistance,
my mother refuses further rehab, subverts nurses
with her twisted mouth, a profane voice
that climbs operatically in anger and despair.
Even after the doctors diagnose brain damage,
pre-existing insanity, urge commitment,
my father cannot sign the papers.

The mere suggestion that she seek help
makes her bare teeth, her eyes flash,
one good arm still agile enough to jerk
tubes out of veins, hurl anything in reach.
She demands her pocket book, the beginning
of a new obsession, as if by holding purse strings
tight enough she can keep her freedom.

This paranoia will continue like a siege,
and while money will become her chief concern,
keeping tabs on me and my father will come
a close second, phone lines crackling with rage,
a one-woman FBI tracking our every move,
time-clocking our lives to the second,
and if the answers don't chime with her busted
inner gears, an acid tongue hysteria returns.
From this moment on, everything –
from flat tires to thunderstorms – will be our fault,
another instance of us bleeding her dry.

Like Patty Hearst, we will adapt, acquiesce,
sometimes sympathize, stop asking why.

My Mother Demonstrates How To Escape From A Plane Crash

Although she has never flown on an airplane, my mother sits on a low stone wall at the entrance to the cemetery and tells me she wanted to move to New York City and become a flight attendant. I am kneeling in green grass in front of a chest of drawers searching for socks not worn at the heel, the sky above us blue and tufted with motionless clouds.

My mother will die never having her stomach drop, never feel ears popping from the altitude, the heaviness that settles into limbs, the shallow breath that comes with thin recirculated air, the way a body adapts to unnatural, human flight.

When she was a girl, a flight attendant was one of the most glamorous jobs in the world. The crisp uniform, jaunty hat, kid gloves and matching luggage all reeked of worldliness, something to benevolently hold over the heads of those other girls who spread legs instead of wings, invited high school sweethearts to climb aboard and permanently ground them.

In this place where I will bury her, my mother stands at attention, mended socks on her hands, and demonstrates the drill she learned from a manual: The exit doors at the front and rear of the plane, and with her arms outstretched as if poised to fly, the escape hatch over each wing.

blowup

Detour

Lee first gave me head
behind an abandoned restaurant
on Virginia Avenue.

It was midnight after seeing *Steel Magnolias*,
crying over poor Shelby's kidney failure,
cautious hand-holding in fagbash suburbia.
I had a Taylor Dayne cassette single in my pocket,
the one he bought me at the mall:
With Every Beat of My Heart.
Love in the last gasp '80s,
riding boys in cars, Z.Cavaricci's around ankles,
Hypercolor t-shirt siren red with lust.

After I filled his mouth too quickly,
I couldn't make Lee come,
my technique not yet perfected,
but I imagine his semen would have tasted bitter,
like those strangers I've since encountered
who held my head, made my throat a receptacle,
God casting out the flood waters, my soft palate
a perfect landing pad for fallen angels.

On a recent afternoon detour,
I do a double-take as I pass the restaurant,
now reclaimed and painted blue, transformed
into an adult entertainment palace called Pleasers.
I think of all those girls on their knees, mouths open,
taking up a ministry I started fourteen years ago.
There should be a sign out back, a marker
next to the electric meter, some small token,
an acknowledgment that I came here first.

Sex In My Parents' House

I was 19 before I had sex in my parents' house. Serious sex, not exploratory masturbation with Bruce, my first best friend, when we were 12 and naked in the woods behind his house. What would Mom and Dad have done if they had found me face down on the living room floor? Lee's ass pumping air, deep drilling, the baby blue shag carpet giving me rug burns. Lee, who I treated badly because he was just a stand in for the one who got away, breath laden with *I love you's* that were more than just orgasms talking.

Later, I feigned insanity, indifference, incompatibility to make him go away. Could hear the hurt in his voice over the phone and wished I could snatch rejection back down the snake-coiled line twisted like a tourniquet around my arm. No one has ever made love to me quite like Lee did those short months we were together. He was an adult, knew how to please, wanted to please me, tried over and over. My mother liked Lee, said he was pretty, would have forgiven the stains on the carpet, the image of her son impaled on the floor in the room we only used when company came.

I can still smell that carpet, old and dusty with disuse, stretching out before me like a cartoon ocean. I floated upon it, disembodied, seeing what my parents might see from the doorway. The truth they had always known, no longer at the edge of their thoughts, but overtaking them like a baby blue shag tidal wave.

Bare Back

Your bare back made me stop.
Hitchhiker, nineteen and blistering,
only walking to the store.
How about a diversion, I live just next door.
You must know what I stopped you for,
I feel myself slouching toward whore.
It's passed down through maternal genes.
You, shaved head, smooth skin, rock hard.
Me, taking all comers.
I'll have you home in an hour.

Hustling

Bad hooker business sense,
should have collected the cash
before he was gumming my cock,
his old man hands like Mars,
red, raw and cratered,
moving over my lunar surface.

He lured me in with his picture,
taken in some other decade
when guys would have paid him,
but he's over 70 and lonely.
While borderline kiddie porn flashes
across the TV, he kneels arthritically,
joints cracking, pleasure oblivious to pain,
as I try to find the disconnect, pretend
he's a pop star, actor or old lover,
make dollar signs dance behind my eyelids.

But I must be a disappointment to him;
I'm not innocent and dewy with lust
like those boys in the magazines.
I'm pushing 30, my customer is pushing death,
and after I come in his mouth and he jerks off,
I can't take the $200 he peels off a mountain of bills.
I take $20 for gas, hand the rest back to his protests,
kiss him on the forehead like he's my grandfather.
He waves from the door as I pull away,
wondering how I'll pay the electric bill.

Mr. Rogers Made Me Fat

It was after Make-Believe,
when I was vulnerable.
He made the peanut butter
jar appear on his kitchen table
between the Museum-Go-Round
and Daniel Striped Tiger's Clock,
dipped in a spoon, lifted it
to his mouth like sacrament,
proclaimed it good.

Wishing for Someplace Else,
I wanted to please him,
so I scampered to the kitchen,
climbed the counter to the top
shelf and found my first addiction.
As the cold metal touched
my tongue and salty sweet
the roof of my mouth, I was hooked.

The empty jars would stretch
to the moon now, Fred is dead,
and the magic Trolley still runs
on schedule, perpetually empty.
It disappears into a hole in the wall
faster than Lady Elaine Fairchild's
boomerang-toomerang-soomerang,
and I'm too tall and wide to follow.

Freshman Orientation

18/m asian in town for freshman orientation. inexperienced but love to be sucked. don't be to old. staying in dorm so you must have place. – Craigslist personal ad

I become device and vessel made of metal
a receptacle for your youthful stamina

past my sell by date, would lie to your face
if I ever saw it, but I'm down below

where the others won't go, in the dark
with inexperienced fingers in my hair

your eyes clenched, I'm a blank screen
project those skinny boys onto me

my ventriloquy, my scenarios
push you past sore and tender

you tell me about the ones
who came before, carry pictures

they are all young and sculpted
but not always open mouthed

Post

Behind me in line at the PO
Frenchman in blood red shirt twitches
twirls the curl on his forehead with restless
fingers, sucks his teeth, while the clerks
roll necks and eyes at the frustrated sighs
of customers with badly-wrapped packages
clumsily prepared passport papers
argumentative over postage rates.

I can only catch a few words of French:
his hatred for this line, fat Americans
the bitches behind the counter.
My eyes shift to the slacker in front of me
jeans hanging from his ass, shredded hems
three-day stubble, unwashed hair, enquiring
about box rentals for a year.

When he glances over his shoulder
I wink at him, and his face turns guilty red
as if titty mags and dildos are falling
from his pockets. He wants to flee
but the clerk is already explaining terms
handing him a key, her eye on the clock.

That's when I realize Frenchy
is breathing on my neck, sniffing
cologne I dabbed behind my ears.
I look back, and he freezes
eyes half-lidded, says haltingly:
You smell like someone I used to know.

Sex Machines

> *I'm in love, I'm in love with a strict machine*
> – Goldfrapp

Heavy equipment outside my house
peeking in every window, oversized
voyeurs with names like roadheader
pile driver, pipe layer, knuckleboom
bottom dump, bulldozer, backhoe

I've got my back against the cool wood
of the dresser playing hide and seek
while a cherry picker threatens
to take off the tissue paper roof
my skin teenage virgin electric

The idea of exposure and crush
my legs wrapped around unbending metal
sends a ramrod shiver up my spine
all those edges to navigate and climb
or to be lowered into the dirt and mangled

Oh, psychosexual infantilism, oh, paraphilia
you had me at birth, when I was another
object, my homosexuality a deviation on par
with rapists, molesters and humiliation seekers
I take this one for the team, machinery lust

your wrecking ball doesn't scare me

After You Left

These are visible scars:
crescent-shaped impressions
over my knuckles where
the car door slammed shut;
sore at the corner of my mouth
I picked until it left a shadow;
cyst crater in my thigh, dormant
volcano waiting to erupt;
gouge in my shin where
I slipped in the sulfur spring
thinking I could walk on water.

Garland
for John Gilgun

I indulge my homosexuality,
cash in a ticket for a night with Garland
on PBS singing *The Man That Got Away*.
I covet that tight navy suit, that poise.
Maybe it's true: we all want to be her.

I loved Judy when I was a child.
Maybe it's required, inbred, the deal she made
in the afterlife to keep her properly worshipped.
I got tapped young, handed my membership card,
pushed down the yellow brick road toward boys
hiding behind curtains, teasing me
with their secret things.

What I really want to know is how it feels
to sing that way, to be able to open my mouth
and have that beautiful roar issue forth, to plant
my feet and push the music out of my lungs
like some celestial dam breaking open.
To throw my head back and surrender to sounds
I make, instead of singing along with the radio.

Give me one long Cukor take, birth my secret star.
Let me slink through those slicked-backed boys
and their horns. I want to be the one-man man,
undone by my own foolishness.
I'll take her mantle, be the one who falls in love
with the no-goods, the ne'er do wells, the fags,
if I can have a voice that staggers them all
into silence and then into my open arms.

Night 65
for Michael

White on black, letters and numbers
glitter and reflect off headlights,
south into Texas night,
toward San Antonio, where big sky
begins and mercury bubbles.
I am on my way to you,
we haven't met,
but you will appear like a cipher
wearing a communist t-shirt,
a bag inscribed "sexual confusion"
where I spout poetry to uninterested
youth, but not you – ageless and still –
your delicate handshake accelerating
my pulse, tugging at gravity.
You'll find ten dollars and buy my book,
act like you're meeting someone
of consequence, show up the next night
for more, tell me you're a Virgo,
our births one day apart,
then I'll never see you again.
All along the highway, the signs
>			Speed Limit
>				75
>			Night
>				65

as if reduced momentum, ten clicks,
could ever save us in a crash,
spare me from racing into impossible walls.
When I leave three days later,
I will press harder, breaking the law,
speedometer topping 80.

Girl Crush
for Farrah

I grew my hair and feathered it for you,
we were the same shade of blonde.
I had the red bathing suit poster
on my bedroom wall, your smile
a nightlight, signal to noise.

Now I can see that your teeth
were clenched, head thrown back,
not so much playful as predatory,
eyes telegraphing that the tingling
I felt down below was fleeting.

There would be no compromise
after this image. You refused to take
Charlie's calls or jiggle and giggle
your way to stereotype.
That smile said, set me on fire.

Expectations defied burn faster,
consume in a crackling wave.
Love remains but is transferred.
The curve of your breast said,
I am not a mirror. Look elsewhere.

The Virgin Mary Appears
in a Highway Underpass

Mary pops up in the strangest places,
usually as a window stain or sandwich,
but yesterday she dripped down the wall
of a Chicago underpass, brought the faithful
running with candles and offerings, blocked traffic.
I saw the pictures, couldn't see her face,
saw a giant, gaping vagina instead, just failed
my Rorschach Test, going to hell for sure.

If this is Mary, she sure gets around,
recasting herself as a Holly Golightly,
popping up where you least expect her,
causing trouble for the locals.
But why would she choose to appear
in condensation, burnt toast or ditch water runoff?
Some will say it's proof that she still dwells here,
runs like an undercurrent, manifests in the mundane.

I say, cut the parlor tricks, Mary.
If you want a little respect, come flaming
out of the sky on a thunder cloud,
ride it like a magic carpet over Middle America,
speak in a voice like Diana Rigg or Emma Thompson,
command attention instead of this sleight of hand,
a stain to be cleaned with soap and water,
so easily erased.

Why I Want To Be Pam Grier

I want to pull a gun out of my hair
and blow your head off.
I want to wear black leather knee high boots
and plant my ten-inch heel up your sorry ass.
I want to flim you and flam you and just say
goddamn you,
while I slit your throat with my knife.
I want to be exploited, overworked
and underpaid but look damn good doing it,
cause I'm always getting laid.
I want to be an idol, a nobody,
a *whatever happened to her*,
then put on my Kangol hat, my tight black suit,
look better than I did twenty years ago,
and smoke you one more time good and proper.
I want to cross 110th Street with a bag full of cash,
and one last sweet kiss from the man
who actually gave a damn.
I want to drive away into the morning light,
headed for Spain, hurting like hell,
but with my head up
and the taste of him on my lips.

Confirmed Bachelor

Now that I've given up on a ring
happily ever after rocking chair

wet dreams and ex-boyfriend
epiphanies, I repress myself

one cardigan away from 1954
favorite uncle who rarely visits

Internet is the new speakeasy
tiny, sizzling neon arrow pointing

down stairs for doorway
tugs and fumbles, dark bricks

scrape my knuckles as I
surrender to the no name night.

Raise the Titanic

At the bottom of my old toy box
the Titanic is wrecked, listing
between Big Bird and Bionic Woman
red and black paint faded,
stacks cracked, masts long gone.

The night I built her, I bit down
on the crusted glue tip, sealed my lips,
and while my mother screamed in horror,
my father grabbed a toothbrush
to scrape my mouth clean of poison.

The model would never float. It ran aground
on my dresser until it went nose down
into toy graveyard, littered with the forgotten
and outgrown, settled into long dark.

But now that Lillian Asplund is dead at 99,
only five when she huddled in a lifeboat,
her father and brothers sinking un-cinematically
into icy Atlantic, I hold my breath and dive
into the sea of basement damp,
bring the ship back to surface.

I can almost see Lily waiting on deck,
breath hovering like a ghost,
deciding she will never speak of this again,
will disappear into the ether, take memories
hidden in drenched pockets into next lifetime
to be stored in a cool, dry place.

From this depth, I can see my father
looking down at me, his face rippling
in the dank air, smiling, telling me
to go on ahead and not be afraid,
that he'll be on the next boat.

Christmas Day

Dad has gone blind,
every mouthful of food a surprise
as his fork moves uncertainly
over the holiday meal.
He stands unsteadily, waiting
for blood to circulate back to his feet
before shambling back to the living room.
He lingers in front of the old gas heater,
wavers like the blue jets flickering in the grate,
says he's never warm.

Mom is a demented tour guide,
pointing out photos I've seen hundreds
of times in my grandmother's house,
a shrine to Uncle Terry, dead ten years,
who makes the electric lights shimmer
whenever we mention his name.
We exchange unwanted gifts and cash,
find solace in this routine, make excuses
for why it isn't more – the dwindling
social security checks or doctor bills.

Small talk will turn to accusations,
to nitpicking, to shortcomings.
Grandmother will retreat to the kitchen,
put on yellow gloves, plunge into hot dish water
until the air returns to normal, until overfull bellies
sedate us into submission, the need for naps,
so she can usher us out, mission accomplished,
with a forced, *don't be a stranger.*

Mom will say, *it doesn't feel like Saturday,*
because holidays are always inscrutable,
like rooms with no clocks or windows
and time that flattens out into dead air.
We are suspended here, holding our breath,
waiting for the world to spin again on its axis.

Broken Things

My mother hovers now, whipping this world
with damaged blades, her selective amnesia

is rudderless, requires a stabilizing hand
from my father, the elephant who never forgets,

catalogs deceit and desire, reminds her
of shortcomings once every twenty years.

Like when abducted children
appear on the news, left for the taking

at shopping malls by careless parents,
and she swears she would never do that

to her only child. My father thumbs his memory
until he finds dates and times, evidence of me

alone at movie theaters, arcades,
our dark house, watches her lose altitude.

He will never forget her space exploration
when she looped her tether to another,

drifting high in the atmosphere, oxygen thin
enough to blot out our faces, form ice.

When she returns to earth, constant contact
becomes her repentance, radio always transmitting,

and even from this distance I can hear
her distress call, waiting for a message

that I have forgiven her, and I have.
Even broken things can still fly.

My Father Escapes A London Hotel Fire

Although he's never left America, he staggers from the porte-cochere, blinded by diabetes and smoke, arms outstretched, siren clanging in his ears making him deaf. This is how Helen Keller must have looked to Annie Sullivan the morning she arrived in Tuscumbia.

I stand on the street with a girl I've never met named Michelle, for whom I have inexplicable feelings, and we both catch my father as he falls under the arms guiding him through a maze of hoses and gawkers. He sits on steps, breathes heavily through his mouth as fire bursts through the roof. My father grips my hand, rests his head on her shoulder, and her long fingers lightly skim his bald head, shining with sweat.

Later, at another hotel, my father asleep in the other room, I lie on a bed with Michelle, her smooth cheek against my own, curly hair splayed like a halo on the pillow, brown eyes searching my face for any entry point. I love her, want to be inside her, renounce my past life, but we know this will not happen, and when I kiss her, she is a reverse sleeping beauty, dead at my side, turned to ash. One flick and I make her disappear in smoky haze.

I hear my father stir. *I tried*, I say through the open door. Oxygen whistles through his nose: *We're alive, why ask for more?*

resolution

Render
for Sally Mann

> *Take a glass plate and clean it well*
> *In the light, fill the center with collodion*
> *Tilt until it reaches each corner*
> *Pour the excess back in the bottle*

Your darlings are poison
candy cigarette daughter
another hung from a tree
son waist deep in rising water
they float in mercury time

> *Take the plate into a dark place*
> *Immerse in silver nitrate*
> *Dry off the backside and load it into a dark slide*
> *Place into the camera and expose*

In the back of your truck
hands become stained, toxic
outside is Antietam night
where collodion once held wounds
ground exhales the centuries
the moon turns silver to blood

> *Develop using a ferrous sulfate*
> *Fix the plate with potassium cyanide*

Decomposing body
eye socket and earth merge
skin a leather handbag
jawbone and cheek dust
pillow for the dead head
in brutal Knoxville heat

> *Time is essential in wet-plate photography*
> *Move quickly to a portable darkroom*
> *Rinse the plate in fresh water then dry*
> *Varnish with sandarac, alcohol and lavender oil*

And the children again, older
freckled lunar landscapes
postmortem stillness
the boy's eyes fixed and dilated
three perfect funeral masks

> *Note that a blue sky and clouds are impossible to render*
> *Expect imperfections and subtle debris*

Acknowledgements

Thank you to the editors of the following publications in which these poems first appeared (sometimes in slightly different form):

Assaracus: "Physical Education" and "First Blackmail"

Atlanta Review: "Barney Rubble Saves Our Lives"

Blaze: "Why I Want To Be Pam Grier"

Blue Fifth Review: "After Adultery" and "Squelch"

Chiron Review: "Garland" and "Wonder Woman"

Contemporary American Voices: "Raise the Titanic"

Floating Bridge Review: "Sex Machines"

MiPoesias: "Hustling"

Motel 58: "Night 65"

Muse Apprentice Guild: "Trivial Pursuits"

New Delta Review: "Ian"

The Other Voices Project: "Christmas Day"

poeticdiversity: "To Margot Kidder, With Love"

Poetz: "Parallel Lines" and "Funtown"

Scythe: "Freshman Orientation," "After You Left" and "Girl Crush"

Slow To Burn (MetroMania Press): "Freedom Train" and "The Virgin Mary Appears In A Highway Underpass"

Tears in the Fence: "My Mother Demonstrates How To Escape From A Plane Crash" and "My Father Escapes A London Hotel Fire"

Terminus: "Three Mile Island"

The Next Best Book Blog: "Tuscumbia, Alabama"

Ugly Mug Anthology: "Blowing Rock, NC"

Velvet Mafia: "Bare Back" and "Sex In My Parents' House"

This collection would not have been possible without the invaluable input from these amazing poets and friends: Kate Evans, Cherryl Floyd-Miller, Karen Head, Tania Rochelle, Jackie Sheeler, Megan Volpert and Cecilia Woloch. I must also thank Bryan Borland and the Sibling Rivalry Press family for their love and support in crafting the final version of *Render*.

About the Author

Collin Kelley is the author of the novels *Conquering Venus* and *Remain In Light*, which was a 2012 finalist for the Townsend Prize for Fiction. His poetry collections include *Better To Travel, Slow To Burn* and *After the Poison*. Kelley is also the author of the short story collection, *Kiss Shot*. A recipient of the Georgia Author of the Year Award, Deep South Festival of Writers Award and Goodreads Poetry Award, Kelley's poetry, essays and interviews have appeared in magazines, journals and anthologies around the world. He lives in Atlanta, Georgia. For more information, visit www.collinkelley.com.

About the Press

Founded in 2010, Sibling Rivalry Press is an independent publishing house based in Alexander, Arkansas. Our mission is to develop, promote, and market underground artistic talent—those who don't quite fit into the mainstream. We are proud to be the home to *Assaracus*, the world's only print journal of gay male poetry. Our titles have been honored by the American Library Association through inclusion on its annual "Over the Rainbow" list of recommended LGBT reading and by *Library Journal*, who named *Assaracus* as a best new magazine of 2011. While we champion our LGBTIQ authors and artists, we are an inclusive publishing house and welcome all authors, artists, and readers regardless of sexual orientation or identity.

www.ingramcontent.com/pod-product-compliance
Lightning Source LLC
LaVergne TN
LVHW041345080426
835512LV00006B/628